A Robbie Reader

Gardening For Kids

A Backyard Flower Garden for Kids

Amie Jane Leavitt

Mitchell Lane
PUBLISHERS

P.O. Box 196
Hockessin, Delaware 19707
Visit us on the web: www.mitchelllane.com
Comments? email us: mitchelllane@mitchelllane.com

Mitchell Lane PUBLISHERS

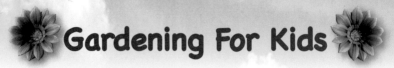

Gardening For Kids

A Backyard Flower Garden for Kids
A Backyard Vegetable Garden for Kids
Design Your Own Butterfly Garden
Design Your Own Pond and Water Garden
A Kid's Guide to Landscape Design
A Kid's Guide to Perennial Gardens

ABOUT THE AUTHOR: Amie Jane Leavitt is an accomplished author and photographer. She graduated from Brigham Young University as an education major and has since taught all subjects and grade levels in both private and public schools. In addition to teaching, she has written dozens of books, articles, games, puzzles, and activity books for kids. She has traveled the world gathering information for her writing and capturing beautiful images with her camera. In fact, she took most of the photographs used in this book. One of Amie's favorite hobbies is gardening. She grows her own vegetables, herbs, and flowers every year and never tires of watching the tiny seeds come to life in her garden. Amie hopes more young people will discover the joys of gardening and gain a desire to care for the earth's precious resources. For this particular book, she'd like to thank her nephew, Isaac, for assisting with the gardening projects and agreeing to be photographed.

PUBLISHER'S NOTE: The facts on which the story in this book is based have been thoroughly researched. Documentation of such research can be found on page 46. While every possible effort has been made to ensure accuracy, the publisher will not assume liability for damages caused by inaccuracies in the data, and makes no warranty on the accuracy of the information contained herein.

Library of Congress Cataloging-in-Publication Data
Leavitt, Amie Jane.
  A backyard flower garden for kids / by Amie Jane Leavitt.
    p. cm. —(Robbie reader. Gardening for kids)
  Includes bibliographical references and index.
  ISBN 978-1-58415-633-8 (library bound)
  1. Flower gardening—Juvenile literature.
2. Backyard gardens—Juvenile literature.
I. Title. II. Series.
  SB406.5.L43 2008
  635.9'62—dc22
                                    2008002255

Printing 1   2   3   4   5   6   7   8   9

                                    PLB

Contents

Words in bold type can be found in the glossary.

Introduction

When it's warm and sunny outside, there are many things you could do. You might choose to ignore the sparkling sunshine and stay cooped up in the house all day. Or you could start a new hobby in the great outdoors. If you like to play in the dirt, you could choose the hobby of gardening, and you would get to grow your very own plants.

If you choose to do so, you're in luck, because the purpose of this book is to introduce you to the hobby of gardening. As a gardener, you'll join thousands of people around the world who enjoy growing their own plants. While this book will teach you how to grow flowers, gardening isn't limited to plants with fragrant blossoms. Some gardeners like to grow vegetables. Some like to grow herbs. Others even like to grow cacti and other desert-dwelling plants.

Gardening is a fun activity no matter what you decide to grow.

How can a kid like you get involved in gardening? Isn't this something that only adults can do? No! Gardening is really a simple hobby, and this book will give you all the instructions you'll need to get started. First, it will show you how to find the best place to grow flowers and how to prepare a **plot** of land for planting. Then you'll get tips on the types of plants that grow well in sunny places and which ones prefer shady spots. If you don't have a plot of earth in which to plant a garden, don't worry. This book will also give you pointers on planting flowers in window boxes and containers.

So, what are you waiting for? Flip to the next page, and let's get your garden growing!

Chapter
Chapter

1

Where Should Your Garden Grow?

The first step in starting a flower garden is figuring out where you want to plant it. For this, you'll definitely need the help of your parents. After all, it's their yard, and they might not want to have flowers growing in the middle of their lawn! You'll also need to get their permission before you start digging.

When choosing a spot, there are a few general guidelines to follow. You should choose an area that is as flat as possible. Usually, hilly areas are harder to keep watered. Areas that have low spots, or valleys, tend to pool water, which will make your garden too soggy. Just remember, flat is best.

Be sure to find an area that isn't exposed to a lot of wind. Wind can harm plants in two ways. First, it will dry them out. Second, if the wind is too strong, the plants will break. If you can't find a flat spot in your yard that doesn't receive too much wind, try planting near a fence or other structure for protection.

Once you've chosen your garden spot, the next step is to mark out how much land you want to have for a garden. For beginners, it's best to stick to a smaller area. If your garden is too large, it will be difficult for you to care for it. The garden can be any shape you desire. It can be a long rectangle or a small square, or even a triangle or circle if you prefer. Use small wooden stakes and string to mark off the area you want for your garden. You could even stretch out a garden hose to form the shape you want.

Now you need to prepare the land for planting. Does the area have grass or weeds growing on it? If it does, you'll need to remove them before you can plant your garden. Your flowers need their own space in which to grow, and weeds and grass in the plot will take the **nutrients** (NOO-tree-unts) in it from your plants.

To remove the weeds and grass from your plot, you'll need several tools: a shovel, a hoe, a rake, and plastic or paper bags (or a recycling bin). Use the shovel to dig into the earth and loosen the soil under the grass and weeds. Be sure to go down deep enough to get their roots.

Garden Tip

Shovels, hoes, and rakes are made in kid sizes too. You can also find kid-sized gardening gloves at a garden shop to protect your hands.

Grass roots do not grow very deep, but weed roots do. Cut small sections, then grab the grass and pull the section up. Shake as much soil off the section as you can. Once you've pulled up your sections of **sod**,

It's hard work removing sod for a garden plot. Sections of sod can be very heavy since one small piece contains thousands of blades of grass and all their roots. Ask your friends and family to help you with this part of your garden project!

look at your yard to see if there are any spots where grass is needed. Grass can be **transplanted**, and it will start growing again in the new place. Be careful to take only the grass and a thin layer of soil, since you won't want to transplant weeds. Rake up the weeds and scoop them into the bags or recycling bin. If your town has a **green waste program**, put the bags or bin of weeds on the curb for pickup, or have your parents help you take them to the city's drop-off bins.

When your plot is cleared of all plants, fluff up your soil and prepare it for your garden flowers. With

Isaac takes his yard waste to his city's drop-off bin. The city will grind the plant material into mulch. Many people put mulch on their gardens. It adds nutrients to the soil, keeps the soil moist, and helps stop weeds from growing. Using mulch is a great way to recycle.

After Isaac removed the sod from his garden plot, he hoed the soil. Hoeing helps remove all the plant roots from the area. It also fluffs up the soil, making it easier for your plants to grow.

Isaac used a rake to make his garden plot level. He also added some bagged topsoil so that his plants could get the necessary nutrients.

the hoe, strike the earth to about four inches deep. Keep doing this until all the soil is loose and fluffy. Then use the rake to smooth out the soil and make the garden plot level. Make sure the soil is soft and dark brown, not hard, dry, or pale gray. If it isn't soft and dark brown, you may need to add some topsoil. This is the nutrient-rich soil that is naturally found on the top layer of the land. Sometimes wind and water will **erode** the topsoil. When that happens, the soil needs to

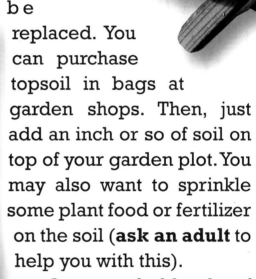

be replaced. You can purchase topsoil in bags at garden shops. Then, just add an inch or so of soil on top of your garden plot. You may also want to sprinkle some plant food or fertilizer on the soil (**ask an adult** to help you with this).

It was probably a lot of hard work preparing your plot, but now you can move on to the fun part—planting the flowers.

Chapter

Chapter

2

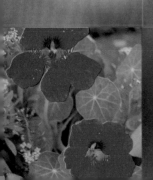

What Should You Grow?

How will you choose which plants to grow? Not all plants are the same. Some plants, called **annuals** (AN-yoo-uls), grow for only one year, while other plants, called **perennials** (puh-REH-nee-uls), will grow for several years. Some perennials may die back in the winter, but they'll return the following spring. You might want a few of each type in your garden.

Plants also require different things to grow. Some plants like a lot of sun, while others grow best in the shade. Some plants need to be watered every day, while others need very little water. Sandy soil is best for some plants, while rich, **fertile** (FER-tul) soil is better for others. Sun, **climate**, and soil are the main things to consider when deciding what to grow in your garden.

Look at your garden spot. Does it get a lot of sun during the day, or is it mainly in the shade? Then look at the soil. Is it sandy, or is it rich and fertile? Figuring this out can be a little tricky. You may need an adult to help you determine what type of soil you have. The last part to think about is what type of climate you have in your area. Do you have long, warm summers? Or is your growing season short? Is it hot and dry, or is it rainy where you live? Once you've answered these questions, you'll have a better idea of the types of plants you'll be able to grow.

Garden Tip

Some sunflowers can grow to be real giants. The tallest sunflower on record was found in the Netherlands in 1986. A person there grew a sunflower that was over 25 feet tall! The largest face on the sunflower belongs to a plant grown in 1983 in British Columbia, Canada. It grew to be over 32 inches wide.

One way to find out about the types of flowers that will grow in your area is to visit a local greenhouse or garden shop. The people who work at these shops can help answer questions about the types of plants you want to grow in your garden.

It is also important to choose plants that are **native** (NAY-tiv) to your area. Often, plants that are not native can become **invasive** (in-VAY-siv)—they multiply and grow quickly because they don't have any natural predators in the new areas. An example of an invasive plant is kudzu. This plant is native to Asia. It was introduced into the United States in 1876. People used it as a ground cover. However, once planted, it is nearly impossible to control—one plant with its climbing vines can grow up to 100 feet long! Now kudzu is considered a plant pest. It grows one

foot a day and can cover trees, power lines, and even cars (if left parked long enough).

The rest of this chapter describes sun-loving and shade-loving flowers. Each of the plant descriptions will tell you what type of soil the plants need. The plants listed here are not the only ones from which you can choose. There are literally thousands and thousands of different types of flowers in the world.

Sun-loving Flowers

Sunflowers are probably the most common of all the sun-loving flowers available to plant in your garden. These flowers come in many types. You can plant tall sunflowers with large leaves and wide faces, or you can grow smaller sunflowers that can be cut and put into vases. Colors range from traditional yellow and

Flowers You Might Like To Grow

Sunflowers	Pansies
Cosmos	Impatiens
Bachelor's buttons	Monkey flowers
Marigolds	Tulips
Alyssum	Snapdragons

Alyssum

Bachelor's Button

Cosmos

Marigolds

Pansies

Monkey Flower

Snapdragons

Tulip

black to pink, white, red, and brown. Another fun thing about growing sunflowers is that you can eat the seeds. Birds like the seeds too. In fact, you might be able to attract more birds to your yard if you plant sunflowers. Sunflowers are quite easy to grow because they can live in rich soil, sandy soil, and many other soil conditions. Just toss some seeds into an empty plot of land and watch them grow!

Cosmos are another type of flower that love the sun. These flowers come in many different colors and heights. There's even one type of cosmos called chocolate cosmos—it smells like real chocolate! Another type is called seashell cosmos. Its leaves are tube-shaped, making it look like a seashell. There are many great things about cosmos. First, it grows the best in poor soil. That's terrific news if your soil is sandy and has very few nutrients. The second is that it grows well in windy conditions. Cosmos also need very little water. This makes it an easy plant to grow.

Bachelor's buttons are also known as cornflowers and basket flowers. These flowers can grow in just about any type of soil. They are usually blue, but they also come in other varieties such as pink, white, purple, and red. Another fun thing about bachelor's buttons is that you can actually eat them! You can toss them into a salad or steam them with vegetables.

Marigolds are very easy to grow. They also have a fairly long growing season. Some marigolds grow to only 8 inches tall, and other marigolds can grow as tall as 3 feet. Marigolds have a strong scent that most animals do not like. If you have a problem with garden pests or cats, these flowers will keep them away from your garden. Marigolds come in a wide variety of colors, ranging from orange and yellow to brown and red. Marigolds should be grown in soil that drains well.

Alyssum is a ground cover, which means the flowers are very short and the plant spreads out over the soil. There are more than one hundred different types of alyssum in such colors as white, pink, lavender, and violet. Alyssum can grow in just about any type of soil, even rock gardens. Not many insects or diseases will bother this plant, which makes alyssum an easy flower to grow. Try planting it around the outside of your garden to make an attractive border.

Shade-loving Flowers

Pansies are a favorite plant for shade gardens. The flower looks like it has a face. Pansies come in many different sizes and colors, including red, purple, blue, pink, black, yellow, and apricot. They can be solid or have up to three colors on each flower. Pansies prefer cool weather. They grow best in rich soil with plenty of nutrients.

Impatiens are quite easy to grow, as long as they are given the right conditions. They like warm weather, but they don't do well in direct sunlight. They definitely grow best in shady areas that get morning sun. Impatiens also need plenty of water and rich soil. They come in many different sizes and colors.

Monkey flowers come in over 150 different types. When you squeeze the bottom part of the flower, the pattern of colors inside looks like the face of a monkey. These flowers do best in swampy conditions, so you would need to give the plant plenty of water. Monkey flowers grow well in just about any type of soil.

Tulips are grown from bulbs instead of seeds. In the northern hemisphere (HEH-mis-feer), the bulbs are planted in the fall. After the bulbs rest

Flower gardens can be grown around backyard ponds. Adda is showing the tallest flowers in her garden: columbines. When she planned her garden, she decided to plant her sunflowers elsewhere. She didn't want her pond in the shadow of six-foot-tall sunflowers!

underground during the cold winter months, their flowers bloom in the spring. Tulips grow best in cool, moist soil that has plenty of nutrients.

Snapdragons are another fun flower. If you put your fingers inside one of these flowers, you can move it up and down to look like a mouth. Snapdragons come in many different colors and sizes. They can grow in partial shade, but they also do well in full sunlight. Snapdragons do best in rich, fertile soil.

Chapter

Chapter

3

Butterflies, Birds, and You

Did you know that some flowers will attract butterflies to your garden and others will attract hummingbirds? There are even some flowers that you can eat. You may want to study these types of flowers to see if you want to add any of them to your garden.

Flowers That Attract Butterflies

Butterflies are attracted to flowers that have sweet **nectar**. This is the juice that flowers make. Bees use nectar to make honey, and birds and butterflies drink nectar for their food. Just as people use baths and feeders in their yard to attract birds, you'll need to provide butterflies with a tasty nectar meal if you want them to come to your garden.

There are many plants that attract butterflies. A few of them are buddleia (butterfly bush), French marigolds, peonies, hollyhocks, coneflowers, petunias, nasturtium, and daylilies.

Flowers That Attract Hummingbirds

Hummingbirds use their long, tubelike beaks to get to the nectar in flowers.

Hummingbirds
especially love the
color red. If you
want to attract
these little winged
friends to your
garden, focus
on planting red
flowers.

They love many different flowers, bushes, trees, and shrubs. Some of these plants are monkey flowers, nasturtium, snapdragons, foxglove, daylilies, and impatiens. Plant these flowers in your garden, and you're sure to have tiny hummingbirds fluttering from plant to plant all over your yard.

Flowers You Can Eat

You may have never imagined that just like butterflies and hummingbirds, people can actually eat flowers from the garden too! You have to

You can plant peppers and other small vegetables in your flower garden too. Peppers are particularly pretty because they have shiny skins and come in many different colors (red, green, orange, purple, yellow). They will add a striking accent to the delicate blossoms in your flower garden.

Some people like manicured gardens with perfectly pruned plants, but other people like more natural-looking gardens of wildflowers.

remember, though, that not all flowers can be eaten. In fact, some flowers could make you very sick. Even if a flower is okay to eat, sometimes people spray their plants with chemicals to kill bugs. You wouldn't want to eat those plants, either. It's very important that you never eat a plant unless you first ask an adult if it's safe.

Garden Tip

It's also fun to grow vegetable plants in your flower garden, or flowers in your vegetable garden. Some pretty vegetables to plant with flowers are peppers, eggplants, and tomatoes.

As you already know, you can eat the seeds from sunflowers. Many people eat these as snacks at baseball games or other sporting events. You can also eat the petals from bachelor's buttons and pansies. Other types of flowers that are **edible** (EH-dih-bul) include dandelions, lavender, violets, hibiscus, carnations, chives, plumeria, basil, nasturtium, and marigolds.

Edible flowers can be used for many different purposes in cooking. People use these flowers in salads. They also cook with them or use them as decorations on cakes. Some flowers can be soaked in hot water to make herbal teas. Chamomile, rose, and dandelion tea are all made using flowers.

Chapter
Chapter **4**

Planting Time

Now that you've learned about different types of flowers, it's time to plant your garden. Bulbs and seeds are sold in packets at garden shops. The packet contains a lot of useful information. It tells when to plant the flower in your area. It tells how much sunlight and water the plants need. It also tells how far apart you should place the plants in the garden and how tall they will get. All this information is very helpful. If you follow the directions on the packets, your plants should grow healthy and strong.

After you've chosen your seeds and bulbs, you'll need to sketch out a garden design. Why is this important? Some plants grow really tall. If they are placed right next to a short plant, the short plant will not get enough sunlight and will die. Tall plants need to be placed in the back of the garden. Some types of plants spread out and need plenty of room to grow. You don't want to place the seeds

Isaac took a notepad with him to the garden shop. He compiled a list of flowers that he wanted to grow. Then, he wrote down information about each type. He answered such questions as: When should I plant them? How tall do they grow? What kind of soil do they need? Later, he used this information to decide what types of plants would be best for his garden.

of these plants too close together, or they will not get enough nutrients from the soil. The seed packet will tell you how far apart to plant your seeds.

Here is a sample garden design. Notice how the sunflowers are placed in the back. The shorter flowers are placed in front of these. Alyssum is a

ground cover, so it is used as a border for the garden. You don't have to follow this plan. Come up with your own ideas and make your garden a unique **floral** creation. But when you make your plan, be sure to use the seed packet information and space the plants the correct distance apart.

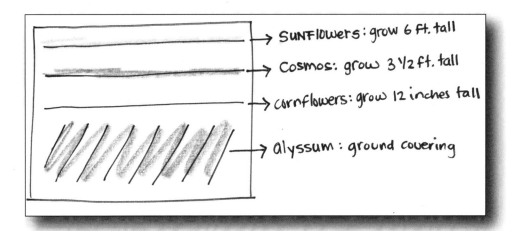

> Sunflowers: grow 6 ft. tall
> Cosmos: grow 3 ½ ft. tall
> cornflowers: grow 12 inches tall
> alyssum: ground covering

Once you figure out where all your flowers will be planted, it's time to get the seeds in the ground. For this, you'll need to use the hoe again. Starting at one end of the garden, make a shallow line in the soil with the hoe. This is your first row. Mark it with a stake and label it with the flower's name that you want to plant here. Then, use your diagram to see how far away the next row must be. Measure the distance, and make your next row. Keep measuring and marking until all the rows are complete. (For some designs, the rows do not have to be straight.)

If you don't want to start plants by seed, you can always transplant them. Isaac bought some marigolds at the garden shop. He dug a small hole in his garden, placed the flower in the hole, and covered its roots with soil.

Carefully open one of the seed packets. Be sure not to spill any of your seeds—some flower seeds can be tiny. Plant the seeds and cover them according to the directions on the seed packet. Follow these directions for each row.

After the seeds are planted, sprinkle them gently with water. If it rains really hard on your newly planted plot, your seeds might wash away. Check the local weather forecast to make sure you'll have a string of sunny days before you plant your garden.

Make sure to keep the soil moist for the first few days so that your seeds can **germinate** (JER-mih-nayt), or sprout. You don't want to give them too much water; if you do, the roots could turn moldy and rot. A light sprinkling of water once a day for the first week should be plenty. After the first

You can start your seeds in containers instead of planting them directly in the soil. Be sure to follow the same directions for watering, wherever you start your seeds.

week, follow the directions on the seed packet for the correct amount of water to use. Remember, flowers such as cosmos don't need a lot of water, while impatiens do. You'll need to learn about each plant in order to help it grow strong.

The best part about planting a garden is watching the seeds grow into tiny plants. Each plant will grow at different rates. The seed packet will tell you how long it will take for them to germinate. Some take only seven days, while others might take fifteen or more.

Throughout the summer, you'll need to maintain your flower garden by weeding it. If you don't keep

Your flowers will stay pretty on the plants for only so long. Then they will begin drying and making seeds. This is a natural cycle of the plant, but it takes a lot of energy. In order for your plants to keep blooming, you must remove the blossoms that are going to seed. This process is called deadheading.

Isaac discovered that he had to spend time weeding once a week or his garden was a mess. After his first time weeding, he realized that it was too hot during the middle of the day to work in the garden. He did his gardening chores in the morning and evening hours instead.

the weeds out of the garden, they will use up too much of the soil's nutrients, and your flowers will die. Don't just pull anything out of the garden, though. You may want to ask an adult to help you determine which plants are weeds and which plants are flowers. After you've had more experience gardening, you will be able to spot weeds a lot easier.

Eventually, your entire garden plot will be covered in a blanket of green. Then flowers will bud and bloom, and your garden will be just as pretty as you imagined it would be.

No Space? No Worries!

Many people live in houses that don't have backyards. They may live in a big-city apartment building or housing complex. Some people may have a backyard, but there isn't room for a garden. Does this describe where you live?

If so, don't worry. You don't need a plot of land to have a garden. As long as you have a little sunshine, water, and soil, you can grow plants just about anywhere. You just have to be creative.

One way to grow plants on your windowsill is to use an old soup can. **Ask an adult** to wash it first to get out all the old food. (Be careful of sharp edges.) Then fill it halfway with soil. Gently place one flower seed in the can and put a little bit of soil on top. Sprinkle the soil with water, and place the can on your windowsill. In a week or so, you'll have a tiny plant growing in the can. Repeat this process with other flower seeds that need the same amount of sunlight, and you'll soon have a flower garden growing on your windowsill.

If you can't find soup cans, think of another kind of container that might work. Yogurt cups or plastic drink cups from restaurants are good containers. So are old pots, baskets, plastic boxes, and tin pails. If you have a balcony or a space in the backyard to

You can plant a variety of flowers in the same container. Just make sure they all require the same amount of sunlight and water.

put containers, you can use larger containers like troughs, buckets, or tubs. People have grown plants in such unusual containers as old shoes, tires, and plastic beach balls cut in half. It's best if your containers have holes in the bottom so that extra water can drain. If too much water soaks the soil, your plant's roots will get soggy and moldy, and the plant will die. If your container doesn't have holes, **ask an adult** to drill or poke holes in it for you.

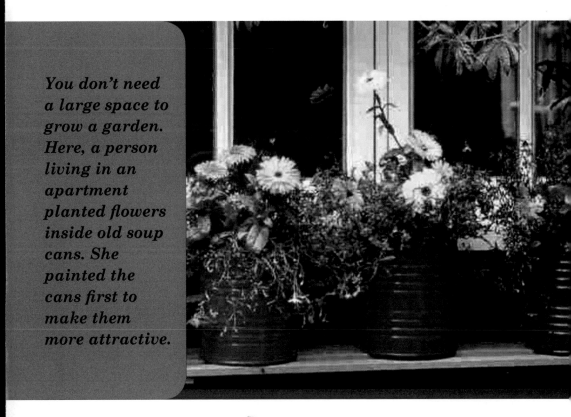

You don't need a large space to grow a garden. Here, a person living in an apartment planted flowers inside old soup cans. She painted the cans first to make them more attractive.

If you live in a hot climate, use light colors for your containers. Dark colors absorb more of the sun's energy, and the containers will cook your plants.

Keep in mind that when the water runs out, it could make a mess. Place a dish under the container if you have it indoors.

Now you can get started on your new hobby. Just remember, the old saying is true: Practice makes perfect. The more you garden, the better you'll be at it. It won't be too long before you're a gardening expert. You just might be able to give new gardeners tips and advice someday too!

Group containers together, or find something interesting in which to display them, such as a garden cart. You can also use an old wheelbarrow, mailbox, bathtub, or similar item. It's handy to display them in something that has wheels so that you can move them easily.

Craft

Decorate a Gardening Belt

When you work in your garden, it's easiest if you have all your tools in one place. That's what makes a gardening belt so great. You can store your seeds in one pocket. You can slip your hand shovel and rake in another pocket. Then, when you're finished gardening for the day, you can attach your gloves to the belt with a clothespin.

You can buy gardening belts at the store. You can even buy a carpenter's belt at a hardware store and use that for your gardening. But instead of just having a plain old belt like everyone else, why not decorate yours into something special?

You Will Need

Plain white-fabric gardening or carpenter's belt

Plain white gardening gloves

Fabric paints and brushes

Old newspapers

Clothespin

Craft

Tips
- Ask your parents if it is okay for you to paint in the house.
- Wear old clothes in case you get messy with the paints.

Directions
1. Layout the newspapers in the area in which your parents said you could paint.
2. Decide what you want to paint on the pockets of your gardening belt. Maybe you want to paint your favorite flower. Maybe you'd prefer painting animals or insects. You could even paint pictures of fruits or vegetables.
3. Using a brush, paint a picture on each pocket. Be careful not to smear the paint with your hand as you go on to the next pocket.
4. Paint a picture on the back of each glove. This is the side that will go on the top of your hand, not on your palm.
5. Let the paint dry completely.
6. Fill the pockets with your gardening tools, seed packets, and other supplies.
7. Use a clothespin to attach your gloves to the belt.

Further Reading

Books

Bradley, Clare. *Fun With Gardening: 50 Great Projects Kids Can Plant Themselves*. London: Southwater Publishing, 2000.

Bull, Jane. *The Gardening Book*. New York: DK Children's, 2003.

Krezel, Cindy. *Kids' Container Gardening: Year-Round Projects for Inside and Out*. Batavia, Illinois: Ball Publishing, 2005.

Morris, Karyn. *Jumbo Book of Gardening*. Minneapolis, Minnesota: Tandem Library Books, 2000.

Rushing, Felder. *Dig, Plant, Grow: A Kid's Guide to Gardening*. Nashville, Tennessee: Cool Springs Press, 2004.

Web Sites For Kids

National Gardening Association: Kids Gardening
 http://www.kidsgardening.com/

University of Illinois Extension: My First Garden
 http://www.urbanext.uiuc.edu/firstgarden/

Works Consulted

Barron, Pattie. *The First-Time Gardener*. New York: Crown Trade Paperbacks, 1996.

Corey, Kathy, and Lynne Blackman. "A Feast of Flowers." Epicurean.com.
 http://www.epicurean.com/articles/edible-flowers.html

Edwards, Jonathan, and Peter McHoy. *The Seasonal Flower Grower*. London: Anness Publishing Ltd., 2004.

Gardening with Perennials. Cincinnati, Ohio: Horticulture Books, 2004.

Grey-Wilson, Christopher. *Annuals & Biennials*. London: Dorling Kindersley Publishing, Inc., 2000.

Roth, Susan. *Complete Guide to Flower Gardening*. Des Moines, Iowa: Better Homes and Gardens Books, 1995.

Strong, Graham, and Alan Toogood. *The Mix & Match Color Guide to Annuals and Perennials*. Millers Point, New South Wales: Murdock Books, 2000.

Water, Denver. *Xeriscape Plant Guide*. Golden, Colorado: Fulcrum Publishing, 1998.

Further Reading

On the Internet
Better Homes and Gardens
   http://www.bhg.com/bhg/gardening/index.jsp
Garden Guides, Your Guide to Everything Garden
   http://www.gardenguides.com/
Home & Garden Television Online
   http://www.hgtv.com/hgtv/gardening/
National Gardening Association
   http://www.garden.org/
Suite 101: Flower Gardens
   http://flowergardens.suite101.com/
Sunset Magazine Online
   http://www.sunset.com/sunset/

Glossary

annuals (AN-yoo-uls)—Plants that live for just one year (one growing season); new seeds must be sown for the same type of plant to grow the next year.

climate (KLY-met)—The type of weather an area usually gets.

edible (EH-dih-bul)—Safe to eat.

erode (ee-ROHD)—Wear away; wash away.

fertile (FER-tul)—Soil that is rich in nutrients, which makes it able to produce healthy crops.

floral (FLOR-ul)—Having flowers.

germinate (JER-mih-nayt)—To start to grow (as from a seed).

green waste program—Programs run by cities and towns to collect plant wastes and grind them into mulch.

invasive (in-VAY-siv)—A living thing that is introduced to an area from somewhere else. Because it has no natural predators in the new area, it is able to take over the area from what already lived there.

native (NAY-tiv)—A living thing that grows naturally in an area.

nectar (NEK-ter)—The sweet juice produced in flowers.

nutrients (NOO-tree-unts)—Chemicals that help things grow.

mulch—A substance made up of plant waste used to add nutrients to the soil, prevent water from evaporating from the soil, and stop weeds from growing.

perennials (puh-REH-nee-uls)—Plants that continue to grow from one year to the next.

plot—A small area of ground for planting.

sod (SOD)—A section of grass and soil that is removed from the ground.

transplanted (trans-PLAN-ted)—Removed from the soil in one area and replanted in another; the roots must be included for the plant to continue to grow.

Index